MW00891308

CANCER PARTY!

WRITTEN + ILLUSTRATED BY SARA OLSHER

mighty + bright

COPYRIGHT © 2018 SARA OLSHER
ALL RIGHTS RESERVED.
PUBLISHED BY MIGHTY + BRIGHT
MIGHTYANDBRIGHT.COM

For my daughter, Charlie;
my parents, Susan + Neil;
my partner, Bear;

and Brandi,
Aunt Lois,
+ Bonnie

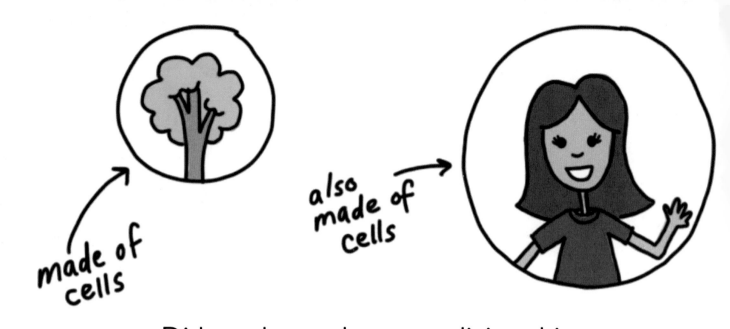

Did you know that every living thing is made up of tiny little guys called cells?

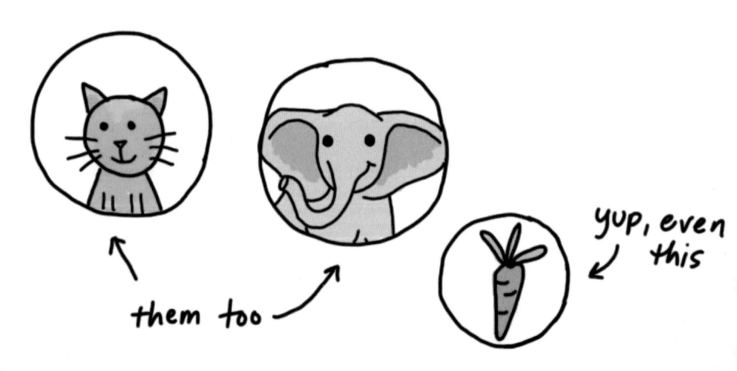

Cells are like blocks, but they put **themselves** together. (Whoa, right?)

We are cells! We are <u>soo</u> tiny, you can't even see us. But we are what bodies are made of.

One very cool thing about cells is that one cell can **make** another cell anytime it wants.

That means that cells can
build and build and build . . .
It's like building with LEGO
and **never** running out of blocks!

imagine the tower you could build!

Every cell has a job.
Together they build body parts,
then tell them how to work.
They make hearts pump,
legs walk, and lungs breathe.

Hi! We are skin cells!

We are blood cells!

And we are heart cells!

Hey, thanks guys!

Without them our bodies wouldn't work **at all.**

And having a healthy body is basically the best thing ever!

A healthy body can run, jump, swim and play.

But every once in awhile, one of the cells forgets what its job is. It can't remember what to do! It's so confused.

And since it doesn't know what else to do,
it decides to have a **PARTY**.

It's really lonely at the party, though, because all the other cells are working.

But remember, it knows how to make friends.

So it does.

It splits in half and makes a friend, and
then that cell makes a friend,
and **that** cell makes a friend.
Before long, it's
a big party!

**A CANCER
PARTY.**

There's just one problem:
A cancer party isn't very healthy for the body.

No one at the party is doing their job. Soon the party gets so big, it starts to crowd out the guys who **are** doing their jobs.

And that's no good! We need all our cells to do their jobs so our bodies work right.

When someone finds a cancer party in their body, they definitely want to get it out. We want our bodies to stay healthy and work perfectly.

So how do we get a cancer party **out**?

To get the party out, usually a doctor can give someone surgery. This means the doctors will make the person go to sleep at the hospital, then carefully take the party out with a tiny knife. The person doesn't feel anything.

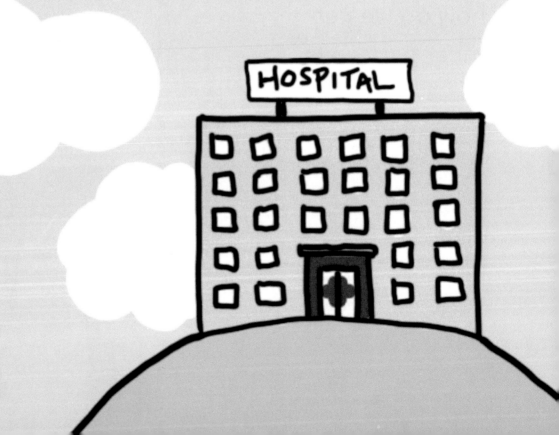

Once the cancer party is out of the body,
the other cells in the body are happy!
Every single cancer cell is gone, and
they can make the body work right.

Doctors need to get all the cancer cells out of the body, and sometimes surgery isn't enough - especially if the cancer cells packed up their pals and traveled to other parts of the body, or if the cancer cells are swimming around in a person's blood instead of hanging out in one spot.

If that happens, doctors can do two things.

Sometimes,
the doctors use a big
machine to zap the cancer cells with a
heat ray called radiation and they all die.

To get radiation, the person lies on a table while a big machine sends out the rays.

They usually have to go to radiation every day for about a month.

Radiation doesn't hurt, but after awhile the person's skin might turn red, like a sunburn. They might also get tired. Both of these things go away pretty quickly.

The doctors can also give the person medicine called chemo, and the medicine kills the cancer cells.

When cancer cells die, the party is wrecked, and all the cells have space to do their job again.

The medicine kills the cancer party,
but it also does some very not-fun things.

One thing the medicine does
is kind of weird and maybe
funny and also sad:
It can make the person's
hair fall out, so they
are totally **bald**.

It also makes
the person
feel tired or sick for
a long time.
They can't run,
jump, or play
like they're used to.

On some days, the medicine
doesn't bother the person so much.
You can take a walk together, drive places
together, read together, or watch movies.

But other days, the person's body might hurt or feel tired. On those days, ask the person how you can help!

They might need a hug - or they might just need to sleep.

Unfortunately, there's nothing you can do to make cancer go away. You didn't start the party (that's impossible), and you can't end it, either.

But you **can** make a person with cancer feel happier, and that is a **very** important job.

And all the hard stuff is worth it when the cancer party is gone! All the cells are doing their jobs, and the body is healthy again.

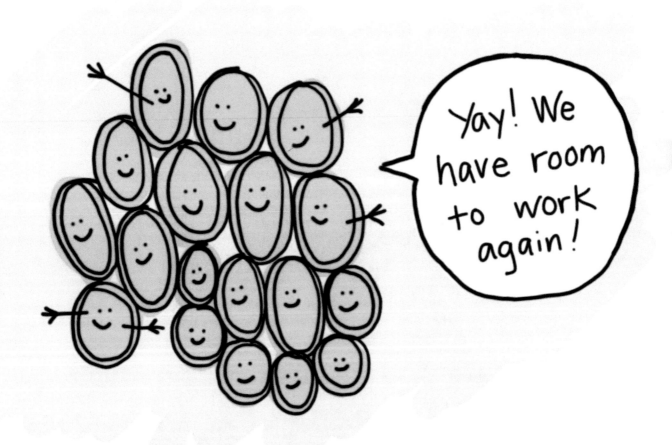

And you know what that means?
A healthy body that can run, jump, swim and
play again . . . and new hair!

More Help
Making Cancer Easier on Kids
from mighty + bright

Magnetic Charts Based on Decades of Science

. . . and created with the help of survivors, therapists, nurses, and grief counselors.

A cancer diagnosis changes your family's routines, which is hard on kids. They want to know that you'll be okay, but they also want to know how cancer affects **them**.

Our charts help kids understand what's happening, and when — which is proven to decrease their anxiety levels.

Learn more on our website: mightyandbright.com/cancer

Make sure kids know they won't be forgotten, with magnets for school pickup and drop off

Schedule our 15 "light activities" — easy enough to do from the couch when you're exhausted

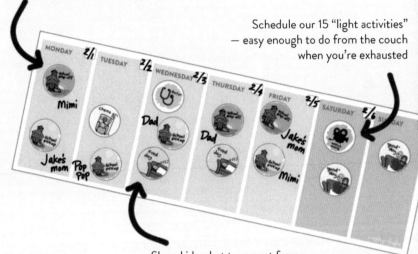

Show kids what to expect from treatment with magnets for "good" days and "tired" days

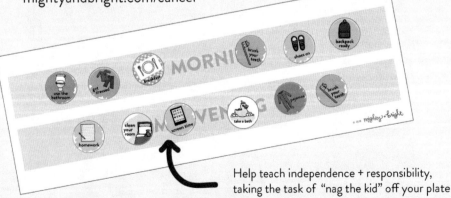

Help teach independence + responsibility, taking the task of "nag the kid" off your plate

www.mightyandbright.com
@mightyandbrightco
MADE IN THE USA

46881694R00015

Made in the USA
Middletown, DE
02 June 2019